Unspeakable Patterns of the House

Eleanor Perry

Flirtation #9

salò press

This collection copyright © 2020 by Eleanor Perry

All rights reserved. No part of this publication may be reproduced, stored in a retrieval system, rebound or transmitted in any form or by any means, electronic, mechanical, photocopying, recording or otherwise, without the prior written permission of the author and publisher. This book is sold subject to the condition that it shall not by way of trade or otherwise be lent, resold, hired out or otherwise circulated without the publisher's prior consent in any form of binding or cover other than that in which it is published.

Some of these poems appeared previously in the following journals: *Tentacular, para·text and Erotoplasty*

978-1-9165021-8-5

Printed and Bound by 4Edge

Cover design and layout by Salò Press
Art by The Miuus Studio
(www.themiuusstudio.com)

Typeset by Andrew Hook

Published by:
Salò Press
85 Gertrude Road
Norwich
UK

editorsalòpress@gmail.com
www.salòpress.com

for the silences

Contents

: in the lumen of the bone defect, there is something like a piano that believes itself to be John Lennon. two cigarette scars on a hazelnut rim. delicate familiarity, like an edited pig's kidney. studies show that a third of those asked would feel uncomfortable if an enemy possessed their hairbrush. two millilitres of napalm. a curvature of waxed feathers. anything can be made sacred. the first mirrors were simply pools of still, dark water.

biologically, pigs are very similar to humans, though studies show that many believe a transplant from a pig would result in the development of piglike qualities. mottle and disruption. split thickness. the outline of a soldier or military vehicle. we look for patterns because we love control. like repeating the word peace over and over while a man with a neuro-develop-mental disorder is administered a lethal injection. like 15-volt increments for every wrong answer. anything can be cursed. *authority wins more often than not* says James Hardy, who just didn't have a heart handy. a little interpretation of bone, as if the mirror kept a portion of each reflection. as if the word *mirror* carried a part of the mirror within it.

: have you ever asked yourself what you
really believe? a granule of innards emitting
habitual blue. a clique of neurons which
echo Pliny the elder, whose memory would
fail him if he did not—from time to time—
hear the same word repeated:

picker. picker.

trick the brain that the body is safe. mark the
torso with brightly-coloured shams. scratch
your tongue with the sharp edge of an
unmilled sixpence. the mirror will steal
anything. a thin layer of nerve-riddled tissue.
a scapular feather. the abrasion of grief.
"chac-chac-chac-chac," sings Pliny, "if i
encounter a word i cannot pronounce, i will
die." he speaks of a beauty that is sufficient,
but the mirror takes whatever is just

enough.

gift of speech a drop of blood, glossy
metallic.

: in giving a name to the relic of an exploded star, let us juxtapose the word *clerical* with the word *psychoanalysis*. gritty little relic like a pebble in the brogue or a language of vignettes and hyperlinks. so-very-British this particular pulsar, stiff in the quartz & fretting its skeezy entrails. some people can glitch right into your happy medium, leaving the remnants to suck up a teaspoon of neutrino pulp heavier than 58 million refrigerators. for instance, a man checks envelopes before posting them to ensure he hasn't carelessly placed his daughter inside. cool story bro, but we've heard it all before from Freud except his version had flowerpots and a clockwork vagina. but wait, let's for a minute assume that not everything wants you dead. glitch interval as the star shudders itself liquid. here, a vortex scenario of doors and other forms of admission. *oh Jeremy Taylor, you old hack, scrupulously eating moths you can't digest.* sure, doubt is wedged in the body like the Large Magellanic Cloud, but in the time it takes to manufacture a kink in the orbit so small and inexact that it cannot correct itself, a committee of highly-efficient business people decide to table the issue and move on.

: let's talk about excess for a minute. the question is not *what*, but *when* to interpret. imagine the household as uninterruptable sequence. a project we might call 'the ultimate guide to sharpening.'

please. my imaginary body is nobody's business, says the old glacial flow on the rim of a Mars impact basin. glial lump. glitter cell. precipitous eye flickering with curriculum. *besides, there is no such thing as* body *in the household*. the perfect edge dominates all others adjacent to it. label the right eye talismanic. and the mouth. and the dune fields. perhaps the happy little crater knows best. excess is a system feeding on itself. a reservoir of self-similar screens. lack of proof as *inability to give substance to*. grattage repetition as unexpected surface.

decal repetition as a glass upon which gouache fractals. *clean your filthy fingers and repeat*, says the Viking Orbiter. i'm not kidding. Mars also has a heart, and a glassy worm. any smooth-surfaced thing pressed lightly creates a squamous quality. ridges, not etched ribs. not glassiness. things eaten-away look shinier than their surroundings. aluminium skin to scrape that glimmer off.

: in a crystal structure, a phase change without dispersal is known as a *military* transformation because the atoms move like soldiers in a bus queue. a *civilian* transformation is one in which there *is* no bus queue. this is not my physics. micrographic pictures of pearlite look like deco palms, thumbprints, a spine, a blood vessel, broken glass pieces.

let's say we get sick collectively. heave our bodies through the day, atoms pulled downwards through the void by their own weight. hyperlapse. telecine judder. drag the shutter to allow more available light in. pacing is a form of movement without purpose. you too could exist as a form of energy inside a jar. flick a switch in your teeth and move so fast that everything else remains still.

a colony in three dimensions is an interpenetrating bi-crystal. but wait, did the study rely on data collected through Amazon outsourcing? did the participants complete tasks for more, or less than, half the minimum wage? substitution splice. telecine wobble. the study asks me to imagine the colony as a cabbage immersed in a bucket of water. what have we learned? maybe that i am not a real-time machine.

: within the boundaries of sleep, an inhabitable void of convex space, in which,   at all times, the potential surveillance of entrances.

partition as the symbol of a tension between the household and the horizon. everything apportioned into pertinent, uncomplicated units.   edges, corners, surfaces, all performing dolorous subjectivities. labelled rooms are, after all, the means by which to keep apart as well as bring together.

in this way, we might understand the verb *to wake* as meaning *to cut open*. Coronis' blazing body, a curved and bird-shaped stroke of the pen to mark an ending. everyone knows that the body has memory. think of consciousness as a smooth and continuously charming seaside village. think of sleep as a seismically-chaotic surge of abyssal water.

or alternatively, Sleep Inertia 2.0, subtitled How Silicon Valley Can Help You Be More Like Newton. shiver your brain up through a series of baroque micro-epilogues. send desolate and accusatory letters to your friends. slither about whispering healing dreams in the ears of learned gentlemen. break off the labyrinth at the throat and unspool it to predict the end of the world. they say violent motion in a void is out of the question but if you imagine yourself as a very special boy chosen by god then anything is possible.

: perhaps you, constant human person, feel like a four-dimensional space-time worm made up of sequential portions. perhaps you feel like a rotted pulse of light reflected from a mirror back towards its own dreadful upwelling. maybe you consider yourself mistaken in the belief that all temporal fragments—lungs, phosphenes, knot-secreted proteins, entrepreneurs like, for instance, business mogul Elon Musk —are all simple three-dimensional items.

it's not a question of *is* or *isn't*. imagine yourself stretched across a hundred years of time. every damn moment a new and obstinate someone, sloughed off in hot pink twangs. a new and creepy little consciousness, unpackaged, flailing, and dying every second. how would you breathe in these accidental skins? this is not my revision. this is not my dummy payload.

Augustine of Hippo insisted that the present is a knife blade placed somehow exactly between. he was wrong; the present is a death-entity running amok in the bio-lab ingesting various drugs. be sure to feed it banknotes if you want a model three sedan in the afterlife.

: you probably don't know why you   suddenly think of
     monarch butterflies   while shopping. the word
      synapse   derives from the Greek meaning
         to clasp together. a kissing
configuration. how many   spheres can kiss passionately
            in four dimensions?
     even your interneurons   are organisms of the
market.   do you love commerce,   my little nasty?
     biological payloads   yield usable data.
Albert II, the first primate   in space, died on
impact,   leaving a 10-foot-wide crater
     in the ground.   the other Alberts—one, three, four,
five—   suffocated, blasted to bits, crashed
     back to earth. even the sixth,   renamed to
     deflect bad luck,   baked in the desert in his
space capsule. it is   in situations such as this that
     a doorknob is a kind of religion. some
things shine like eyes   but are not eyes.
     sea urchins, gypsy moth   eggs, snails, brine
         shrimp, crickets. a well-disciplined
corpse. a tiny, thorn-shaped   stone one twenty-
     fourth of an ounce. we could   make long,
     feathery lists   all day long.   curl
     our toes   one hundred times for
each foot every night,   just like Tesla did.
     accept objects only in   multiples of three.
clean our orifices   for at least twenty minutes.
     autobiographies are, by nature, plastiglomerate. what
holds the debris together is   synthetic and
     malleable.   our cells eat and
they learn to accept.   and a wavering star slits to plasma
     in the x-ray universe where   everything is erratic.

: peel away from yourself. the creepest of feelings is *soft curved armchairs*. a sheet of glass all the time. dream yourself a faulty mechanical shark whose teeth represent enclosure. in the dream, toasters, coffee machines, whisks are types of monument.

you may feel your body dollied forward for maximum silky pull-back. maybe you are reassessing everything you had previously believed. there are boundaries falling from your mouth and fossilizing. Pliny the Elder held that sharks' teeth fell out of the sky during lunar eclipses. the moon, void of its requiem, spit back its oral balustrade in disgust. this kind of refusal is cusp-shaped; a point on the grinding surface. lingual face against the blade of earth's occluding body.

maybe you wake unprepared for a vertigo reflected in the kitchenette's sullen diplomacies. maybe you can't fully bite into the day's slippery flesh with your gummy human language. there is transaction between a sharp edge and its easy dulling, but you cannot shed 35,000 teeth you do not have. a shark's party trick is to turn its u-shaped stomach inside out, a rinsing gesture that the blood moon deeply covets. intolerable nausea of rusted umbrae replicated in the sheen of a retro citrus juicer.

in the watery friction of routine, the moon's incisal edge slides coppery and tired of reflecting.

: red noise [lymph pop] slosh and glops. the water gently [dead leisure]. as oval window bulges in [cochlea spit] ossicle soft, whisper like [definition of ripple]. [aah after] tapered stiff frequency [wet mouth] ribboned skin spilling [fatty white] orbital surface of [leaking] ping-pong mechanism [ditto gum fracture]. polyester dress [um repeating] tangled bone [jaw glint] through aureole portion [moist paste of teeth] gravels pulse glottal [fissure or hiatus] crashing out to [suck on vaseline]. oh an 'old school' kind of oligarch [at the clacking] all pressure at the lungs. deflected between [dark L in lull] red red repulse and [raptor scream of] knife-filled mouth and edit the mouth [too clean]. clicky little bubble such awful [*don't eat an entire cake*] and stick a pen in [*so very glam*] to scrub across [snailish ventricle] for efficient coupling of [fossil lick] at holocene thresholds. the contents of a glass [a *no* where a *yes*] slime and slime and [delicate spider folds] in the image of [red red sever] less than [tender mother membrane].

: alive in […] [burnt bones stuck + red lake] //
soft-bodied, oval […] mouthparts. Susan. viscous.
blocky. carousel of [not all light] […] for glazing
layers — suture slices (echo) Susan (echo) voxel
weighted […] abrupt skeleton. Susan keeps a
record […] (discount stores) […] clotting when
brushed. […] like little hook […] of outer wing
(less) surface. Susan eats at her desk. it is a
continuous — doors ordinarily kept. […] silver
vitreous to […] [make lake madder] […] alum / / it
stained their teeth. […] aquarelle. errors. […]attach
to fabric. Susan says, "eat the household." […] help
the dye bite. […] 100,000 insects, raw &
pulverized. Susan imagines them floating in a […]
bubble […] ERROR404 — a room full of people.
Susan says, "be a detective in your own life." […]
your frappucino. (see all the red residue?) […] there
are other ways to kill bugs. *sicklied* […]*and
enterprises of great pith* […]. little baskets, lipstick
[…] & pastries. *insects happen.* […] Susan says,
"be dark ambient metallic drones & resonances"
[…] she says always act *as if.*"

: at body's periphery, Homeric reminders
of dispersal. how the glass morphs into
nearly rupture. there is little comfort in a
beetle which spits boiling peroxide from its
abdomen, but that does not mean there is
none. 'lucky' ones heaved up glutinous
from 90 minutes in a toad stomach; not all
heroes wear capes. holothurians, for
instance, soften ligaments on a whim and
spill out through the holes, then regrow a
body from what's left: a soap-like foaming,
or details of the mouth. pistol shrimp
secrete smithereens of light from imploding
bubbles. taut bead of glomerida, passive
ooze of juliform. just evolve your muscles
into a small door. tangle ants in your hair.
break from naked bone + puncture your
way to functionality. or possess this lipid
envelope, its sponge + glitz. stand still in it,
disobedient as a frill.

: in the household, windows are mercurial. small eminence of light on the lip as teeth fluoresce. with each mood shift, rehearsal becomes its own infrastructure, these glow-in-the-dark bones a pretty after-thought. this is what it means to be sick of useless souvenirs: an opal kidney, the ancestral ear. the blue light which remains. forms of empathy left rotting in the mud. it is said that we write outwards from the stomach, as if it was part of the forgotten labour of digestion. but these punctured vowels are way too intimate; vestigial lyric re-emitting cardiographic neon like a green eel. better this inelegant schlock of molar pulp + jump scares. a muscular accumulation of talons + ganglia. add a mouth that emerges from the regular mouth. this is exactly what will be considered sexy. Susan says *I am (please fill in the blank)*. she doesn't know the abstraction into which she is woven. + neither do you.

: are you suddenly the blast radius? hot
plush draped briolette (a broken rib, a
furry red) gemmed pineal oozing shatter?
are you the wreck + the wreck (in blood)
+ the bolide unknotting from its radiant?
polysaccharide whump won't pipe down
the plasma to chiffon slurs: you're gasoline
like Hemingway + Poe, you are writing the
next great American concussion. are you
demanding an upgrade from your overseer?
are you sufficiently smearing your home
with ghosts + obscurities? are you. are you.
spilling over? how does the house not hold
you? you are lamellae fizzing FAX ME
FAX ME gunkbaby you are soft cirrhotic
revolutions. this is the pendulum in your
brain. this is *how do you manage your time
effectively*, where the word *effectively* is a
giant petri dish brimming with small
mosses. you may not pretend to be a river,
or a small and mournful neutron star. you
may not offer as proof of efficiency your
continuous state of matter.

: some critics emphasize the brutality of Susan, her voice floating from a tube extending out of an 8-foot-tall box. the moons of Saturn in her eyes: regular satellites with prograde orbits—

(it is decidedly so)

—a backlash against Puritanism's social mainframe, or simply glistening barbiturates in the Houdini storefronts of this kitsch city. fantasia of fake eyeballs + vulnerability diagrams. the doctor is preoccupied. stockpiling cops + dinosaurs; oh *supremo louche moustachio*, is this truly how crime works?

(concentrate + ask again)

in the amygdala, where the light is more radiant + the sleeves of girls are more finely textured, a real wall is broken by the shadows of a half-drawn curtain. five cents for your psychoanalysis, in raised letters that displace its blue liquid; every feeling listed in an Excel spreadsheet. remaking this collisional family in rigid latex + polyurethane, we assume too much.

(outlook is not good)

several of Saturn's moons are geologically dead, their intersecting fractures forming wisps. Susan's lemonade stand has a chaotic rotation. + the outcome has nothing whatsoever to do with her actions.

███████

: how to explain water to fish: the bleaks,
the flukes. how
one eye migrates to the other side
of the body. there are
names written into it: *Felice, Camille.*
an anxiety of
punctilious men vigorously wiping them
away
with their goddamn lexicon.
why *not* simply chew up all the
money + die?
an eager void will wear its emptiness
openly, an
oceanic legacy of vowels that
lack the dark in their bright
silvery ideas. as if
to curate a version of self as meat sliced
across muscle fibres;
bite radius as preferred unit of distance.
what is unsaid is
an unnavigable surface. like a bottle
whose stem curves back into its belly.
what is intimate, between the
water's pleat and light?
soft, slimy shift,
if you pour in still.

: don't assume that something is true just because
feelings.   in Clearwater, Florida, a stain on
the glass façade   of a finance building. an
underpass in Chicago.   a pretzel. a pebble.
dental x-rays, plastered walls. the hind legs of a dog.
in the   act of consecration there is a nebula
to which   dead stars have fastened their
stiff bodies. when   birds fly into windows
it is because they have   seen the
 reflection of the sky and mistaken it   for a future.
our mistake is believing that it is   the bird
who carries death to the household, and not the other
way around. or rather, like   the bird, it is
believing that   the glass has something
 to give. like permission.   or it is in imagining
that a nebula crumpling under   its own weight
 will always signify the   manufacture of
pristine new stars to replace   those that are
extinct, when sometimes   a cloud
is simply a residue or an   obstruction of the light.

17

Crack Study

: bone regalia so full of pollen
giving tongue its waterlily meat

paterfamilias a monstrous butterknife
dull edge tuliped &&sweethearts

drop like oblongs,, like a pasty mass
of english landlords

make your face a finance office—
distance can sometimes be

a husbandry of peach innards,
or a hundred insect daughters which

lull in radium decay chains
gushing atom "feelies"

luscious pulps
rotting bright rotting dials

&&lip shatterings
here's a slit gluon to void my throatglasstube

here's a syllabus of regrettable bird-skin situations
a bureau of slow boiling

: poor phloem, plastic mulch glides
to ketones &&aldehydes

no laryngeal glow
ozone sucking on the poverty line

star blobs && the asphalt's estranged electrons
in the isobars of your bladder

hot carpark germs collecting angsty solar radio
crumbs in blunt symmetry of grout

from house &&house
to half-life in prim parallelograms

&&professor boys are strangely morphed how
grossly, how baroque—

red-legged itch mites in a curved boulevard
in a lengthy ileum

: long cuts evaluated &&folio abrupts
to smeary gleam bucket

kept skin a pre-chewed mastic so scholarly
scraps &&panko slivers

shrilled xerox
rubs partial thumb to foam

or squalid gloss of geometry in membranes
an indication of bone or utensil

these funnelling bathyspheric mouths
full of miracle

turn muscle to lavish turbine
to evening glove

most days a knot,, a splatter on
threshold enamel

where skin means more than the knife
whose language is a tendril

: taking matters into their own hands
into my own hands into your own

pristine rhombs taking charge taking
over the matter taking

over the matter at hand crystal sputnik
taking root taking macho Clorox into

your own hands taking over responsibility
taking initiative for glycol spheres

&&pectins latexed to buttery calculus
taking responsibility for being responsible

or failing that taking a pocket-knife
to the kidney

dig in low down deadbeef
peptides &&circuit-board eaters

we feel queasy on the manicured
commuter belt little gastrins hyped for

guillotining for taking ownership taking the
choke taking the frightful chemicals taking the

business-end taking the weighted cardboard
taking a leading role taking lawful possession

all safe taking our acidity taking our limpid
so fastened shut the gate now wedge it open

24

:

heart is doors open or
slow vinyl of moon stub

mothsuck in mopboard
hogweed in rain gutters

slick rabbit says, *buy a house
love it, let it ruin*

perhaps i am also called 'house'?
i apply myself like a colour, maybe blue

which means throats i mean heraldry
i mean poems instead of glass

i mean 'glass' as in big holes.
i mean 'holes' as in burst open

: dear salvage in tidal lug
so soldierly,, fret glassy armature

lit lucky in pelagic gut
in greenish crosshairs

in a ghosted borough
carbons && collagens hardening

the gristle is an ambassador
a staircase of red palp

always the rushing lobe, the effort
the heat, the love, the metal

always the clotting, the consortium
the housecoat, the slurry

the loops && closed rooms
the flue &&the utterance

: inscrutable light
of free-living yeasts

of zero-gravity hunger
&&soft soft photons

they are thin &&their mouths are finalised
like a scar

in the sauna, in the dishwasher
in the groceries

the dirt melt,, the glassy ocean
don't be sick,, little thread

don't interrupt your heart
for a million years

or a hundred dollars
for the great white fingers of white ghosts

a starfish cancelled out
the terrible smooth pink diameter

of mammal, bird, of hamster ovary
the body contains many kinds of junk science

Eleanor Perry's publications include *Of Parasites & Proximities* (Contraband Books, 2017); *Meat · Volt · Interruption* (Oystercatcher, 2015); and *Venusberg* (Veer Books, 2015). Eleanor edits *DATABLEED* and runs the reading series *DATABLEEDER* alongside Juha Virtanen; and teaches at the University of Kent.